HAPPY EVER CRAFTER

ROBOTS AND ALIENS

ANNALEES LIM

Published in paperback in Great Britain in 2020 by
Wayland
Copyright © Hodder and Stoughton 2018

All rights reserved.

Senior Commissioning Editor: Melanie Palmer
Design: Square and Circus
Illustrations: Supriya Sahai

Additional illustrations: Freepik

ISBN 978 1 5263 0756 9

MIX
Paper from
responsible sources
FSC® C104740

FSC
www.fsc.org

Printed in Dubai

Wayland
An imprint of
Hachette Children's Group
Part of Hodder and Stoughton
Carmelite House
50 Victoria Embankment
London EC4Y 0DZ

An Hachette UK Company
www.hachette.co.uk

SAFETY INFORMATION:
Please ask an adult for help with any activities
that could be tricky, involve cooking or handling
glass. Ask adult permission when appropriate.

Due care has been taken to ensure the activities
are safe and the publishers regret they cannot
accept liability for any loss or injuries sustained.

CONTENTS

Sci-Fi Worlds

A world filled with robots and aliens usually just exists in our imaginations, especially when we think about the future and all the new technologies that have not been invented yet. Future worlds that we see in science fiction stories could be a reality soon!

Extraterrestrial life is a long word for 'aliens' but it simply means not from Earth. Alien life can be the smallest bacteria or microbes that live on meteors or planets. Often, we tend to think of it as little green men with large eyes zooming into our atmosphere in shiny flying saucers. While there is still no evidence for the existence of aliens, it does not stop human beings from trying to find proof. There are many space programmes all around the world, dedicated to learning more about the universe we live in.

FACT!

UFO stands for Unidentified Flying Object. It was used to describe things that flew in the sky but were not birds, aircraft or anything that originated from Earth. People often thought they were alien spaceships but this was never proved.

Robots are real! They are any machine that is programmed by a computer that can carry out tasks with little or no human contact. We have been using robots for years, doing jobs that humans find hard or boring to do. They help make our cars, explore the deep oceans and even get sent into space.

You can have lots of fun making up your own sci-fi worlds. Will yours be filled with giant metal robots that are operated by small, squishy aliens? Or perhaps you will create your own spaceship that you can fly to explore new solar systems. The only limit is your imagination, and this book is a great place to start. Filled with craft ideas, games and lots more, you can become the ultimate space and time traveller using the things you have made that are really out of this world!

TOP TIP

Collect things from around the house for your craft supplies. Old magazines and newspapers make great scrap paper, and don't throw away cardboard tubes, plastic containers, jam jars or old food wrappers – they can all be turned into the fantastic crafts you will find in this book.

OUTER SPACE OUTFITS

Transform yourself into crazy cosmic characters, perfect for any party. These fantastic fancy dress ideas are easy to make by yourself, but are fun to make with your friends, too. You can make these projects really unique by using any spare materials you have lying around.

ROBOT

Robots were built to help humans do the jobs that we find difficult. They are very useful to have around, especially as they don't get tired and never need to stop for food. How helpful can you be when you dress up in your own robot costume?

YOU WILL NEED:

- LOTS OF CARDBOARD BOXES (CEREAL BOXES AND OTHER FOOD PACKAGING ARE BEST) • TIN FOIL
- GLUE STICK • SCISSORS
- TWO STRAWS • SCRAP PAPER
- BOTTLE LIDS • STICKY TAPE OR SILVER DUCT TAPE

1. Make a cardboard head band that is at least 15 cm tall from a flattened box, then cover it in tin foil.

2. Decorate this with scrap paper to make the robot's face. The eyes and mouth should have no round edges.

3. Make some antenna for your headband from two straws and more scrap paper.

4. Lay out lots of flattened card to make a cardboard tabard (tunic) – remember to include a hole for your head. Stick together with sticky tape (or silver duct tape).

5. Decorate the tabard with small card circles covered in foil, lots of colourful bottle lids for the buttons/dials and any other scraps you have.

ALIEN

Aliens come in all shapes and sizes, from little green men to scary sharp-teeth monsters. You can create your own sci-fi style and come up with an alien design that is as unique as you are. Sketch your ideas first and use this project as your starting point.

YOU WILL NEED:

- LARGE CEREAL BOX • SCISSORS • SCRAP CARD • GREEN PAINT • PAINTBRUSH
- WHITE CRAFT GLUE • GREEN TISSUE
- PAPER OR MAGAZINE PAGES

1. Cut off the top of the large cereal box and cut a 'U' shape from the front. Make sure the hole is large enough for you to see out of.

2. Cut out some large eyes on stalks and some antenna from more scrap card.

3. Stick these on to the top and sides of the box using craft glue.

4. Paint the whole thing using different shades of green and leave to dry.

What's an alien's favourite drink?
Gravi-tea

5. Add strips of green tissue paper or magazine pages to the bottom of the box to look like alien tentacles.

STAR TIARA

Stars are made up of burning balls of gas which glow brightly, so we can see them at night. Scientists use colour categories to tell them apart. There are red, yellow and even blue stars. Make your tiara full of colourful stars to match the universe, too.

YOU WILL NEED:

- CARDBOARD / OLD HAIR BAND
- TIN FOIL • STICKY TAPE • LARGE PLASTIC BOTTLE • SCISSORS
- SCRAP PAPER • THREAD

1. Make a cardboard headband or recycle an old hair band. Cover it in tin foil.

2. Ask an adult to cut up a plastic bottle into 5 rings. Cover the edges with sticky tape so that they're not sharp.

3. Use a stapler to attach the rings to the top of the headband.

4. Cut out two identical star shapes that are no bigger than a plastic ring. Cut a slit on the top of one, and the bottom of the other.

5. Slide them together and tape some thread to the middle. Attach to the ring so it spins inside. Repeat to make more stars for the rest of the rings.

DID YOU KNOW?

Our sun is actually a star that is billions of years old. Even though it looks big to us, it is actually one of the smaller stars in the solar system. Other stars look smaller in the night sky because they are further away.

ASTRONAUT JET PACK

There is no gravity in space so it is hard to go in the direction you want when you are floating around. Jet packs (or propulsion units) help astronauts move in space when they are outside the spaceship. Make yours and see how fast it makes you zoom!

YOU WILL NEED:
- TWO LARGE PLASTIC BOTTLES
- NEWSPAPER • WHITE CRAFT GLUE
- STICKY TAPE • PAINT • PAINTBRUSH
- PLASTIC BAGS • SCISSORS • RIBBON

1. Remove the lids from the two bottles and stick together side by side.

2. Cover in torn up pieces of newspaper, stuck down with craft glue, then leave to dry.

3. Paint the bottles white with red stripes and leave to dry.

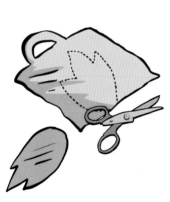

4. Make flames from old colourful plastic bags and stuff them inside the bottle necks. Hold in place with sticky tape.

5. Make some straps so you can wear your jet pack by sticking on long lengths of ribbon (or cut up fabric).

9

PLANET PARTY

If you're planning on celebrating a special occasion with an outer space theme, then have a look at our handy hints. Follow these steps to help you stay organised and remember the most important things you need to make your party a success.

5, 4, 3, 2, 1...
BLAST OFF!
The countdown has begun to the launch of your party and there is lots to get done! Look at this list of things to help you organise and prepare for the event.

5... SPACE! Party themes are a great starting point to help you turn any dull space into a whole new world. You could choose to create your own space station, an alien planet, or even a futuristic version of your house with cool new inventions and gadgets. Find some inspiration with the decoration ideas on page 16.

4 ... A GALAXY OF GAMES! Discover fun new games to play on page 12. You can give out prizes to the winner of each game or keep a scoreboard to see who has won the most games and gets to be crowned the 'Leader of The Universe'.

3 ... ROCKET FUEL! Your guest will need lots of energy to keep up with all the space adventures you have planned. Use the recipes on page 20 for ideas on what to serve.

2 ... GOODY BAGS! Say thanks to your friends who came by giving them a small gift. Look at the craft ideas on page 24 and see what things you can make them.

1 ... SPACE MISSION! Make it your mission to have as much fun as possible. You've done lots of planning and made lots of cool things, so remember to enjoy yourself and have a blast!

INTERGALACTIC INVITES

You have a fantastically futuristic theme but who will you invite? Look at this great Rocket Robot invitation template idea. You could use it to invite your best pals and include all the information they need.

To Space Cadet:

To Space Cadet:
Add your friend's name.

The Countdown has begun to the launch date:
Add the date and times of the party

The Countdown has begun to the launch on ...

Come to the Space Station:

Come to the Space Station:
Add the address of the party.

RSVP:

RSVP:
Ask people to let you know if they can make it.

PARTY GAMES

These simple party games will be a big hit at your party. Easy to make and fun to play, they will keep your guests entertained for hours. Make a Spaceship Scoreboard to keep track of the winners of each game.

COGS AND GEARS

Cogs and gears are wheels that have teeth. They fit together in machines to make things go faster or slower, or have more or less power. They slot together in different combinations of shapes and sizes to make a *gear train*.

YOU WILL NEED:

- MAGAZINES • SCRAP CARD
- STICKY TAPE • PEN • SCISSORS
- GLUE STICK

1. Stick a magazine page picture on to a piece of scrap card.

2. Use the sticky tape roll as a template to draw 5 circles on to the back of the card.

3. Draw square 'teeth' around each circle so that each cog slots into each other.

4. Cut theses out carefully and keep them together in a pile.

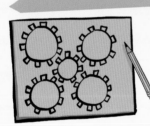

5. Repeat this to make a set of cogs for each player But make sure you choose a magazine page that has a different picture for each player.

HOW TO PLAY

Each player hides another players' set of cogs around the house. Everyone meets back in one place ready for the countdown. After the count of 10 each player goes off to find their set of 5 cogs. When they have found them all, they go back to the meeting place and race to join their cogs in the right order so it makes up the correct picture. The fastest player wins.

SPACESHIP FRISBEE GOLF

Humans have been travelling to space for years but we have only ever landed on the Moon. There is an International Space Station where astronauts can live but it stays in one place and just orbits the Earth, which it does more than 15 times a day. Space programmes are researching how to send humans further into space in the future.

YOU WILL NEED:

- 2 PAPER PLATES PER PERSON
- STAPLER • SCISSORS • PENCIL
- COLOURING PENS OR PAINT
- COLOURED PAPER

1. Cut out a circle in the middle of your paper plate. Use this as a template to draw and cut out an identical-sized circle in the other paper plate.

2. Staple them together to make the spaceship.

3. Decorate with paint or colouring pens.

4. Fold 5 bits of paper in half to look like cards. Decorate each with either a 1, 2, 3, 4 or 5.

HOW TO PLAY

Place the card numbers around a large room or outside space. Stand in one spot and throw your frisbee towards the number 1. If you have not reached it, throw again from where it landed. Count how many throws it takes you to get to the number 1. Stand at the number 1 and throw to the number 2. Count again to see how many throws it takes you. The winner is the person who completes the course in the least throws.

LASER BEAM OBSTACLE COURSE

Lasers are a very powerful beam of light made using mirrors and atoms. We use lasers in lots of machines, to cut things up and even to play DVDs.

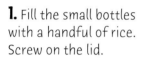

RICE

1. Fill the small bottles with a handful of rice. Screw on the lid.

2. Decorate the bottles with strips of paper, stuck with sticky tape.

3. Cut out lightning bolts from yellow paper and stick them on to the bottles.

HOW TO PLAY

Wind the ribbon or string around things to make an obstacle course. If you're playing outside, you can wrap around trees, and if you're inside you can wrap around chairs or other sturdy bits of furniture. Balance the energy bottles on top of the laser beam strings in different locations. Start the timer and carefully walk through the beams to try and collect the energy bottles. If you knock into too many laser beams at once, a bottle might fall and you will lose a life. The winner is the person who collects the most energy bottles in the least amount of time.

MIGHTY METEORS

YOU WILL NEED:
• LARGE SHEET OF THICK PAPER OR CARD • PAINT • PAINTBRUSH
• SMALL PEBBLES

Most meteors are small bits of rock that have broken off a comet. As they fall from space towards Earth, they usually burn up and can look like shooting stars in the night sky. Any that reach planet Earth without burning up completely are called meteorites – but you'd be lucky to find one!

2. Paint white circles on to the black and add some large and small stars inside each circle.

1. Paint a large piece of thick paper black. An old paper table cloth or a flattened out cardboard box is perfect.

3. Write 10, 20 or 30 on each star.

HOW TO PLAY

Place the board at one end and everyone else stands at the other. Take turns to carefully throw the meteor rocks on to the board. Once all the rocks are thrown, count up the points. 0 points for landing off the board, 10 points for landing in the 10 zone, 20 points for landing in the 20 zone, 30 points for landing in the 30 zone, and minus 10 points for every meteor rock thrown into the black hole in the middle.

4. Paint 5 pebbles in the same colour. Make sets of rocks for each player.

PARTY DECORATIONS

Decorating your party space doesn't need to cost you lots of money to make a big impact. Try these easy crafty makes that are inspired by undiscovered, faraway worlds filled with robots and aliens.

SOLAR SYSTEM HANGINGS

A solar system is made up of planets, moons, asteroids and other things that orbit the Sun. The Sun sits in the middle and everything else rotates around it in a large squished circle, called an ellipse. Our solar system has eight planets, all different in size and look.

1. Cut coloured paper into strips of all the same length. You will need about 20 strips in total.

2. Punch a hole at each end.

YOU WILL NEED:
- COLOURED PAPER • HOLE PUNCH
- SCISSORS • STRING

3. Stack the strips on top of each other and thread a piece of string through one end. Tie a big knot so that the string does not fall through the hole.

4. Fan the strips around in a circle and bend each one into an arch before threading it on to the string.

5. Tie another knot at the top to fix the strips into a globe shape.

FLYING ROCKET SHIPS

Sputnik 1 was the first spacecraft to be launched into space in 1957. Since then, many shuttles, spacecraft and probes have been sent to space with unusual names like Luna, SpaceX Dragon and Helios. Make your very own and add it to the collection. Remember to give it a name, too.

1. Make four tubes by cutting two kitchen roll tubes in half.

2. Cut off the top of a plastic bottle and stick the four tubes inside the hole using sticky tape.

YOU WILL NEED:
- 2 KITCHEN ROLL TUBES • LARGE PLASTIC BOTTLE • THICK CARD
- THIN CARD • SCISSORS • PEN
- WHITE CRAFT GLUE • STICKY TAPE
- NEWSPAPER • PAINT • PAINTBRUSH

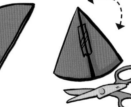

TOP TIP
Hang these up from the ceiling to look like they are zooming through space.

3. Draw four fin shapes from some thick card. Cut them out and stick them to the bottle.

4. Cut half a circle from some thin card and roll it into a cone. Stick to the top of the bottle.

5. Cover the whole thing in a layer of torn up paper and glue, and leave to dry before painting it.

GIANT ROBOT

This robot can be made as big or small as you want. Use lots of small boxes or one giant one to change the look of your robot. You can also cut some holes out of the front of the boxes to hide things in for your guests, or use it as a display for all your birthday presents.

YOU WILL NEED:
- 1 LARGE BOX • 1 MEDIUM-SIZED BOX
- 4 SMALLER BOXES • 2 YOGHURT POTS
- TIN FOIL • WRAPPING PAPER • SCISSORS
- WHITE CRAFT GLUE • COLOURING PENS

1. Cover the largest box in old wrapping paper. If you use the reverse, it will be an off-white colour that you can draw onto afterwards.

2. Stick on some yogurt pots either side, and draw on the face.

3. Take the middle-sized box and cut out the front. Cover this with more wrapping paper.

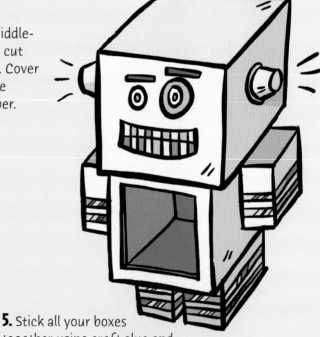

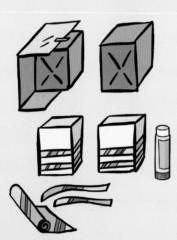

4. Cover the four smaller boxes in wrapping paper and add strips of tin foil as decoration.

5. Stick all your boxes together using craft glue and leave to dry before standing up.

MILK CARTON MARTIAN

The name Martian is a made up word for an alien from the planet Mars, similar to using the word Earthling for people who live on Earth. You can see Mars from Earth without a telescope so keep a look out for a large red star on a really clear night.

1. Cut the top off the milk carton and turn over.

2. Mix together some white craft glue and some green paint.

3. Paint the carton and leave to dry.

4. Use a permanent marker pen to draw on some large alien eyes and slits for a nose.

5. Use a dark green marker pen to add other decorations to the alien head.

TOP TIP

Use a battery operated LED tea light inside the Martian head to make it glow and give an eerie alien feel to your party.

SPACE FOOD

Serve up these spectacular space treats for your guests to enjoy.
Display your fabulous food makes on a table decorated with all
the things you have made. Food labels are a great idea too,
so everyone knows what they are eating (see page 27).

COMPUTER CONSOLE CAKE

The first computer game ever made
was a ping-pong style arcade game
called 'Pong', released by Atari in
1972. Since then computer games
have become increasingly popular,
and moved from arcade halls to virtual
reality games in people's homes.

YOU WILL NEED:

- SQUARE SPONGE CAKE • KNIFE
- DISPLAY BOARD • ICING SUGAR
- WATER • BLACK FOOD DYE
- CHOCOLATE BUTTONS • LIQUORICE
  STRINGS • ICING PENS

1. Mix together the icing
sugar, some water and a few
drops of black food dye.

2. Cut the sponge into one large
rectangle and two smaller ones.
Place them on to a display board.
Cover the sponge in a layer of
icing and press some chocolate
discs into the wet icing to look
like buttons. Leave to set.

3. Cut up some lengths
of liquorice and join the
large rectangle to the
smaller rectangles.

4. Use an icing pen to
add decorations to the
cake. You can add more
buttons, lights and a logo.

LASER BLASTER JELLY

This sonic space shooter is straight out of the films of the 1940s, the Golden Age of Science Fiction. These films grew in popularity as people became increasingly fascinated with the real life Space Race, where countries were trying to be the first to travel into space.

1. Cut the plastic bottle in half and stick to a baking tray. You may need to roll up some newspaper and stick it to the outside so that it doesn't tilt over.

2. Fill the two halves of the bottle with the jelly mixture and leave to set.

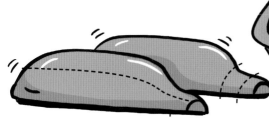

3. Turn out the jellies and cut into sections.

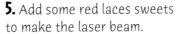

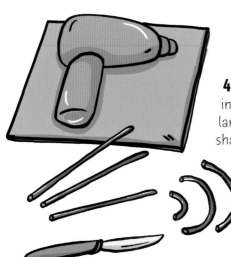

4. Reassemble the pieces in a different order on a large plate to make the shape of a laser blaster.

5. Add some red laces sweets to make the laser beam.

BLACK HOLE CHOCOLATE PUDDING

A black hole is sometimes made when a star is dying. It has so much gravity that it pulls lots of things into it, even light, which is why you can't see it. A really big black hole is called a supermassive. It can only be found using special equipment.

YOU WILL NEED:

- CHOCOLATE PUFF CEREAL • 1 BAR OF DARK AND MILK CHOCOLATE
- CLING FILM • 6 SMALL POTS
- SPOON • WHISK • 1 POT OF CREAM CHEESE • 2 TBSP ICING SUGAR
- 1 SMALL CAN OF CONDENSED MILK

1. Slightly crush chocolate puff cereal with the back of a spoon. Add melted dark chocolate and mix well.

2. Line 6 pots with cling film and spoon some of the chocolate mixture in.

3. Press the mixture into the sides so that you make a cup shape and leave to set in the fridge.

4. Whisk the cream cheese, icing sugar, condensed milk, and melted milk chocolate together and pour into the cereal cups. Leave to set in the fridge.

5. Tip out on to plates and remove the pot and the cling film before serving.

OATY ALIEN EGGS

Do robots have brothers?
No, just transistors

This alien egg recipe is a perfect sweet treat that is also healthy for you. It will give you lots of energy so it is a really great way to refuel after a busy day of space exploration.

YOU WILL NEED:

- DESICCATED COCONUT • 4 TBSP OATS
- 2 TBSP HONEY • 1 TBSP RAISINS
- 1 TBSP DRIED BLUEBERRIES OR CRANBERRIES • 1 TSP VANILLA EXTRACT

1. Place the oats, honey, raisins, berries and vanilla extract in a bowl and mix well.

30 MINUTES!

2. Put in the fridge for about 30 minutes.

3. Split the mixture into 10 and roll into egg shapes.

4. Roll in some coconut and place in a tray.

5. Keep in the fridge until you are ready to serve.

CRAFTY MAKES

Gather together all your space junk and transform them into fun gifts, decorations or even prizes for the games you have been playing.

ALIEN ABDUCTION

Who will you choose to beam into your spaceship? Use a photo of someone you know and trap them in the beam of light to create this 3D photo frame.

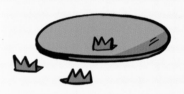

YOU WILL NEED:
- TWO PAPER BOWLS • CARDBOARD
- GREEN PAPER • GLUE STICK
- SCRAP PAPER • SCISSORS
- PLASTIC CUP • PHOTOGRAPH

1. Cover a cardboard base in green paper. Add paper tufts of grass, too.

2. Use a glue stick to sandwich together two paper bowls.

3. Decorate the bowls with scrap paper to create the spaceship.

4. Stick the plastic cup on to the bottom of the spaceship.

5. Cut out the photograph and place it inside the cup. Place the spaceship on to the grass.

LITTLE GREEN MEN

This slime recipe can be moulded, squished and squashed into any shape you like. Add some googly eyes to what you make to create an army of slimy aliens.

1. Mix the craft glue and bicarbonate of soda in to a bowl with 1 cup of water.

2. Add a few drops of green food dye and mix.

YOU WILL NEED:

- 1 CUP OF WHITE CRAFT GLUE
- 1 TSP BICARBONATE OF SODA
- 1/2 CUP SHAVING FOAM
- 1 TBSP CONTACT LENS SOLUTION
- GREEN FOOD DYE • GLITTER
- WATER • BOWL • GOOGLY EYES

3. Pour in the contact lens solution and mix until it turns into slime. You may need to add more solution.

4. Turn out and knead well. Add the shaving foam to make it fluffier.

5. Add the glitter before you start to shape it into the little aliens.

ROBOT PETS

Choose your favourite animal to model into a robot. This project is to make a puppy but you can turn any animal you like into your perfect pet!

YOU WILL NEED:
• TWO SMALL CARDBOARD BOXES
• TIN FOIL • GLUE STICK • 1 KITCHEN ROLL TUBE • SCRAP PAPER • SCISSORS

1. Cover the two small boxes in tin foil like you are wrapping a present.

2. Cut up the kitchen roll tube into four equal pieces and cover with tin foil.

3. Stick the four tubes on to the bottom of one of the boxes, and stick the other box on top of that.

WOOF!

4. Mould more tin foil to make a tail and an antenna. Glue on to the front and back of the boxes.

5. Cut out bits of scrap paper to decorate the body. Make eyes, a nose, ears and robot buttons.

SHOOTING STAR POP-UP CARDS

Use this simple pop-up craft to make party invitations, food name plates, or even a thank you card for the people who came to your party.

YOU WILL NEED:
- TWO PIECES OF COLOURED CARD
- SCISSORS • GLUE STICK • COLOURED PENS

1. Cut out two pieces of coloured card, one slightly smaller than the other.

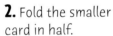

2. Fold the smaller card in half.

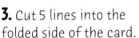

3. Cut 5 lines into the folded side of the card.

4. Bend the cut section and open up.

5. Press the cut section in on itself and then glue on to the large piece of coloured card.

ROCKET PORTHOLE

YOU WILL NEED:
- PENCIL • THIN BLACK CARD
- SCISSORS • PAPER PLATE
- SILVER PAINT • PAINTBRUSH
- COLOURED PAPER

1. Use a pencil to draw around the paper plate on to a black piece of thin card.

2. Carefully cut out the bottom of the plate, leaving the rim intact.

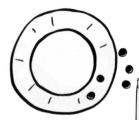

3. Cut out small circles from the leftover black card and stick around the plate rim.

What did the alien wear to his job interview?

A space suit

4. Paint the paper plate silver and leave to dry.

5. Cut out stars and planets from coloured paper and stick to the black card. Glue the silver rim on to the black card, too.

SPACEMAN SALT PAINTING

The atmosphere in space is very different to Earth's, so it is important to protect astronauts when they travel. A spacesuit is essential to wear as it pumps in oxygen to breathe and is thick enough to stop the body freezing. It is also flexible so that the astronauts can move easily.

1. Draw a picture of an astronaut on to the black card.

2. Trace over this picture by squeezing glue directly out of the bottle.

3. Sprinkle salt over the glue and gently shake off the excess salt.

4. Water down some paint and make sure your paintbrush has soaked up lots of the mixture.

5. Gently dab the paintbrush on to different areas of the picture and watch the paint spread. Repeat with other colours and see how they mix when they meet.

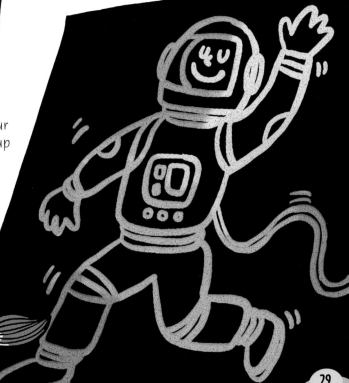

29

PLANET PRINTING

Did you know that until recently Pluto was thought to be the ninth planet in our solar system. It is now just called a dwarf planet. Scientists are still looking for planet number nine in our solar system, which they think could be ten times bigger than Earth. Can you predict what it will look like?

1. Scrunch up sheets of newspaper.

2. Evenly spread some paint on to the pallet using a paintbrush.

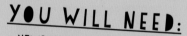

YOU WILL NEED:
• NEWSPAPER • PAPER • PAINT
• PAINT PALLET • CARDBOARD TUBE
• PAINTBRUSH • SCISSORS • BLACK
PAPER • COTTON BUD • GLUE STICK

5. When both sheets of paper are dry, cut the planet print into a circle and stick on to the black paper using a glue stick.

3. Use the scrunched up newspaper and cardboard tube to print paint on to the plain piece of paper. Use different colours of paint to make your planet unique.

4. Spread some white paint on to the pallet and print small stars on to the black paper using the cotton bud.

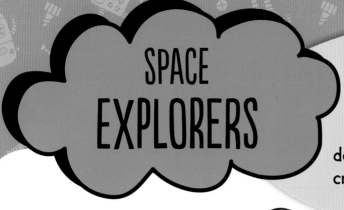

SPACE EXPLORERS

Make a team of space explorers to travel the universe. Use the same technique to make the base of each explorer but decorate each one differently to create aliens, astronauts and robots.

1. Half fill the yoghurt drink pot with the small stones or rice.

2. Use the sticky tape to fix the ping pong ball onto the top of the pot.

YOU WILL NEED:

- SMALL YOGHURT DRINK POT
- PING PONG BALL
- SMALL STONES (OR RICE)
- TISSUE PAPER • STICKY TAPE
- CRAFT GLUE • PAINTBRUSH
- PAINT • BLACK MARKER PEN

3. Water down some craft glue and use this to stick on torn bits of tissue paper to the whole of the pot.

4. Once it is dry, decorate your character using different colours of paint.

5. Add any details such as eyes or outline features using the black marker pen.

SPACE PUZZLE
CAN YOU FIND THE ANSWERS TO THESE QUESTIONS?

1. How many stars can you find?

2. Which spaceship is the odd one out?

3. Who has the most eyes?

4. Which spaceship has the most fins?

ANSWERS: 1. 17 stars 2. D 3. C 4. B

32